EXPLORING THE STATES

Alabama

THE HEART OF DIXIE

by Lisa Owings

BELLWETHER MEDIA · MINNEAPOLIS, MN

Note to Librarians, Teachers, and Parents:

Blastoff! Readers are carefully developed by literacy experts and combine standards-based content with developmentally appropriate text.

Level 1 provides the most support through repetition of high-frequency words, light text, predictable sentence patterns, and strong visual support.

Level 2 offers early readers a bit more challenge through varied simple sentences, increased text load, and less repetition of high-frequency words.

Level 3 advances early-fluent readers toward fluency through increased text and concept load, less reliance on visuals, longer sentences, and more literary language.

Level 4 builds reading stamina by providing more text per page, increased use of punctuation, greater variation in sentence patterns, and increasingly challenging vocabulary.

Level 5 encourages children to move from "learning to read" to "reading to learn" by providing even more text, varied writing styles, and less familiar topics.

Whichever book is right for your reader, Blastoff! Readers are the perfect books to build confidence and encourage a love of reading that will last a lifetime!

This edition first published in 2014 by Bellwether Media, Inc.

No part of this publication may be reproduced in whole or in part without written permission of the publisher. For information regarding permission, write to Bellwether Media, Inc., Attention: Permissions Department, 5357 Penn Avenue South, Minneapolis, MN 55419.

Library of Congress Cataloging-in-Publication Data

Owings, Lisa.
Alabama / by Lisa Owings.
    pages cm. – (Blastoff! readers. Exploring the states)
Includes bibliographical references and index.
Summary: "Developed by literacy experts for students in grades three through seven, this book introduces young readers to the geography and culture of Alabama"–Provided by publisher.
ISBN 978-1-62617-000-1 (hardcover : alk. paper)
1. Alabama–Juvenile literature. I. Title.
F326.3.O85 2014
976.1–dc23
                                        2013002356

Printed in the United States of America, North Mankato, MN.

Table of Contents

Where Is Alabama?

Alabama is nestled in the heart of the southeastern United States. Its **fertile** land covers about 51,701 square miles (133,905 square kilometers). Alabama shares a long border with Mississippi to the west and Georgia to the east. Rivers flow across the state's northern border with Tennessee. Alabama's southeastern border touches Florida.

Southwestern Alabama dips into the warm waters of the **Gulf** of Mexico. Dauphin Island sits at the mouth of Mobile Bay. This narrow island protects the Alabama coast from crashing waves. Montgomery is the state capital. It lies near the center of the state along the Alabama River.

Tennessee

Mississippi

N

W E

S

Birmingham

Alabama

Georgia

Alabama River

Montgomery

Florida

Mobile

Mobile Bay

Dauphin Island

Gulf of Mexico

History

Native Americans lived in Alabama long before Europeans arrived in the 1500s. The Spanish, French, and British fought over the land into the late 1700s. Then the newly formed United States claimed Alabama. The state played a large role in the American **Civil War** of the 1860s. A century later, the **civil rights movement** had its roots there.

Spanish explorers meet with Native Americans

Alabama Timeline!

1519: Spanish explorers arrive in Mobile Bay. Later they search the Tennessee River valley for gold.

1783: The newly independent United States now controls Alabama.

1819: Alabama becomes the twenty-second state.

1861: Alabama joins the Confederacy. This was a group of southern states that wanted independence from the rest of the country. Their actions led to the American Civil War.

1865: Slavery ends in Alabama. However, African Americans are still not treated fairly.

1955: Rosa Parks is arrested for refusing to give up her bus seat to a white man. This leads to a fight against laws that keep black people separate from white people.

2005: Alabama native Condoleezza Rice is the first African-American woman to become Secretary of State.

2005: Hurricane Katrina hits Alabama and other states along the Gulf Coast.

Confederate soldiers

Rosa Parks

Condoleezza Rice

The Land

Alabama's land slopes from low mountains in the north to the sea in the south. The Appalachian Mountains fan out from the northeastern corner of the state. Their rounded peaks and valleys cover much of Alabama. Snow sometimes dusts them during the state's mild winters. The Tennessee River runs west through the Appalachians. Then it loops back toward Tennessee.

The Coosa and Tallapoosa Rivers flow southwest through thick forests. They join to form the Alabama River, which continues through the coastal **plain**. It rushes into the Mobile River before emptying into Mobile Bay. Swamps and **bayous** break up the coast. White sand beaches draw visitors during Alabama's warm summers.

Mobile Bay

Alabama's Climate

average °F

spring
Low: 54°
High: 74°

summer
Low: 71°
High: 90°

fall
Low: 56°
High: 76°

winter
Low: 39°
High: 57°

Did you know?

Severe storms with strong winds often hit the Alabama coast in summer and early fall. In 2005, Hurricane Katrina caused widespread damage and flooding.

The Black Belt

cotton field

The Black Belt is a band of fertile plains that stretches across central Alabama. It is named for its rich black soil. Cotton used to be the main crop grown in the Black Belt. That changed in 1915 when a pest called the boll weevil destroyed much of the cotton crop. Today this land supports forests, livestock, and a variety of other crops.

boll weevil

Alabama

N

W E

S

Black Belt

The term *Black Belt* is also used to describe the region where **slavery** was once common. Southern **plantation** owners needed workers to tend their fields. African people who had been sold into slavery were forced to work on these lands. The Black Belt is still an important part of the state's geography and history.

Wildlife

Alabama's forests, swamps, and rivers are home to many animals. Foxes, coyotes, and bobcats hunt small prey throughout the state. In southern Alabama, nine-banded armadillos dig their burrows in soft soil. Black bears roam the forests and swamps near the Mobile River.

Alabama skies are dotted with bluebirds, hawks, and mockingbirds. Egrets, ducks, and other water birds thrive in swamps and rivers. Swamps and bayous are home to deadly alligators. Other dangerous reptiles include rattlesnakes, copperheads, and water moccasins. Catfish fill the rivers, and shellfish are common in coastal waters.

copperhead

alligator

egret

fun fact

Nine-banded armadillos can jump up to 4 feet (1.2 meters) into the air when startled!

nine-banded armadillo

The U.S. Space and Rocket Center is one of Alabama's most popular attractions. Huntsville is home to this giant space museum. Visitors can explore real spacecraft, enjoy space-themed rides, and tour NASA's nearby research center. People of all ages can also attend the center's famous Space Camp.

U.S. Space and Rocket Center

Talladega
Superspeedway

The Birmingham Zoo is another popular landmark. It has around 800 animals from all over the world. **NASCAR** fans head for the Talladega Superspeedway. It is one of the world's fastest racetracks. Many people stop by a red brick church on Dexter Avenue in Montgomery. Martin Luther King, Jr. once preached and planned civil rights protests there.

Montgomery

Montgomery became Alabama's state capital in 1846. Civil rights leader Martin Luther King, Jr. was a **minister** there in the 1950s and 1960s. Montgomery was also where Rosa Parks started a protest against bus **segregation**.

Today Montgomery is home to more than 200,000 people. It is the second largest city after Birmingham. Montgomery lies in the Black Belt farming region. Many people in the city work for the government. In their free time, people can tour the **capitol** building, visit museums, or attend concerts.

Martin Luther King, Jr.

Alabama State Capitol

fun fact

Six blocks of downtown Montgomery make up a history museum called Old Alabama Town. It shows what life was like in Alabama during the 1800s.

Working

Cotton farming has always been important in the Alabama countryside. Farmers today also grow peanuts, pecans, and corn. Others raise cows or chickens. Forests now cover much of the land that was once used to grow cotton. Lumber from these forests is used to make wood products. Along the coast, workers drill for oil and natural gas.

Factory workers in cities make iron and steel. Others produce chemicals, clothing, and aircraft. Most people in Alabama's cities have **service jobs**. Many of them work for the state government. Others work in hospitals, banks, or office buildings.

Where People Work in Alabama

government
16%

services
70%

farming and
natural resources
3%

manufacturing
11%

Playing

Alabamians love to get outside and enjoy their state's warm weather. People who live near water often go boating with friends. Waterskiing is one of the state's most popular sports. The beaches along the Gulf Coast are favorite places to soak up the sun. Alabama also has several state parks where people hike, camp, and fish.

Car racing events attract fans from all over the state. The Talladega Superspeedway is the place to see exciting NASCAR races. The state has no professional sports teams, but Alabamians are serious about college football.

fun fact

Alabamians are big fans of Crimson Tide football. The team's mascot is an elephant called Big Al.

Big Al

Robert Trent Jones Golf Trail

Did you know?

Alabama is a great state for playing golf. The Robert Trent Jones Golf Trail offers 468 holes on 11 different golf courses.

Food

crab cakes

Did you know?
Fried green tomatoes are a favorite southern side dish. Slices of unripe tomatoes are seasoned, coated with cornmeal, and then fried.

seafood soup

Alabama's flavorful southern meals feed the soul as well as the belly. The Gulf Coast is famous for its seafood. Crabs, shrimp, and fish are always freshly caught. Seafood soups and stews are favorites. Alabamians also enjoy crab cakes and fried seafood dishes.

Barbecue is big in Alabama. Slow-cooked ribs, smoked ham, and other pork dishes are proudly served throughout the state. Native American foods such as pumpkin, corn, and beans can be found in many Alabama dishes. Grits are made of ground corn. They are often eaten for breakfast or as a side dish. Pumpkin, sweet potato, and fruit pies are **traditional** desserts.

Fried Green Tomatoes

Ingredients:

4 to 6 green tomatoes

salt and pepper

cornmeal

bacon grease or vegetable oil

Directions:

1. Slice the tomatoes into 1/4 to 1/2 inch (1/2 to 1 centimeter) slices.

2. Sprinkle with salt and pepper.

3. Dip in cornmeal and fry in hot grease or oil about 3 minutes or until golden on bottom.

4. Gently turn and fry the other side.

Festivals

Mardi Gras

Mardi Gras is a major celebration in Mobile, Alabama. The streets are filled with brightly decorated floats for weeks. People crowd in to catch beaded necklaces thrown from the floats. Mobile also hosts the BayFest music festival each October. More than 125 performances are crammed into a single weekend.

The city of Opp hosts the Rattlesnake Rodeo each spring. An eastern diamondback rattlesnake show is the main event. In October, Alabamians head down to the Gulf Coast for the Annual National Shrimp Festival. They feast on shrimp, listen to live music, and shop for arts and crafts.

fun fact

Mobile was the first city in the United States to have a *Mardi Gras* celebration.

The Montgomery Bus Boycott

Rosa Parks

After slavery ended in Alabama, segregation became a problem. African-American **activist** Rosa Parks helped change that. In 1955, she was riding a crowded bus through Montgomery. The driver asked her to give up her seat to a white man. Rosa Parks did not move. The driver had her arrested.

Bus on which Rosa Parks refused to give up her seat

A few days later, Martin Luther King, Jr. helped organize a **boycott**. He and many others agreed to stop riding Montgomery buses. The boycott lasted more than a year. It led to new laws that ended segregation on buses. Alabamians today are proud of their state's role in the fight for equal rights.

Fast Facts About Alabama

Alabama's Flag

Alabama's flag is white with a red X. It was adopted in 1895. The design is similar to the Confederate flag, which has a blue X on a red background.

State Flower
camellia

State Nicknames:	The Heart of Dixie The Cotton State
State Motto:	"We Dare Defend Our Rights"
Year of Statehood:	1819
Capital City:	Montgomery
Other Major Cities:	Birmingham, Mobile
Population:	4,779,736 (2010)
Area:	51,701 square miles (133,905 square kilometers); Alabama is the 30th largest state.
Major Industries:	farming, forestry, manufacturing, services
Natural Resources:	oil, natural gas, lumber, fertile soil
State Government:	105 representatives; 30 senators
Federal Government:	7 representatives; 2 senators
Electoral Votes:	9

State Animal
black bear

State Bird
yellowhammer

Glossary

activist—one who takes action to support a cause

bayous—small, slow-moving streams that connect to other bodies of water

boycott—a group's agreement not to deal with a person or business

capitol—the building in which state representatives and senators meet

civil rights movement—the effort to gain equal rights for African Americans; the civil rights movement took place in the United States in the 1950s and 1960s.

Civil War—a war between the northern (Union) and southern (Confederate) states that lasted from 1861 to 1865

fertile—able to support growth

gulf—part of an ocean or sea that extends into land

minister—a person who leads religious ceremonies in a church

NASCAR—the National Association for Stock Car Auto Racing; a stock car is a regular car that has been changed for racing.

native—originally from a specific place

plain—a large area of flat land

plantation—a large farm that grows coffee, cotton, or other crops; plantations are mainly found in warm climates.

segregation—keeping certain groups of people apart; African Americans were once forced to go to different schools, use different bathrooms, and sit in different sections of the bus than white people.

service jobs—jobs that perform tasks for people or businesses

slavery—a system in which certain people are treated like property

traditional—relating to a custom, idea, or belief handed down from one generation to the next

To Learn More

AT THE LIBRARY

McDonough, Yona Zeldis. *Who Was Rosa Parks?* New York, N.Y.: Grosset & Dunlap, 2010.

Somervill, Barbara A. *Alabama.* New York, N.Y.: Children's Press, 2008.

Tarshis, Lauren. *I Survived Hurricane Katrina, 2005.* New York, N.Y.: Scholastic, 2011.

ON THE WEB

Learning more about Alabama is as easy as 1, 2, 3.

1. Go to www.factsurfer.com.

2. Enter "Alabama" into the search box.

3. Click the "Surf" button and you will see a list of related Web sites.

With factsurfer.com, finding more information is just a click away.

Index